On Your
Plate

Beans and Nuts

Honor Head

A⁺

Smart Apple Media

Smart Apple Media
P.O. Box 3263, Mankato, Minnesota 56002

Printed in the United States

Published by arrangement with the Watts Publishing Group Ltd, London.

Created by Honor Head and Jean Coppendale: Taglines
Design: Sumit Charles; Harleen Mehta, Q2A Media
Picture research: Shreya Sharma, Q2A Media

Picture credits
t=top b=bottom c=center l=left r=right m=middle

Cover Images: Shutterstock and Istockphoto.
Nikolay Okhitin/ Shutterstock: 4, Travellinglight/ Istockphoto: 5, Varyaphoto1000/ Dreamstime: 6, Travellinglight/ Istockphoto: 7, Vera Bogaerts/ Shutterstock: 8, Kevin Renes/ Shutterstock: 9, Karma_Pema/ Istockphoto: 10, Pierdelune/ Shutterstock: 11, Liudmila Korsakova/ Shutterstock: 12, Creacart/ Istockphoto: 13, Antonio Espárraga/ Shutterstock: 14, Jaroslaw Grudzinski/ Shutterstock: 15, Benedamiroslav,Branislav Senic/ Dreamstime/ Shutterstock: 16, Glenda M. Powers/ Shutterstock: 17, Jumpphotography/ Istockphoto: 18, Maksymilian Skolik/ Shutterstock: 19, Mvp64/ Istockphoto: 20, Drue T. Overby/ Shutterstock: 21.

Library of Congress Cataloging-in-Publication Data

Head, Honor.
  Beans and nuts / Honor Head.
    p. cm. -- (On your plate)
  Includes index.
  Summary: "Provides a basic introduction to beans and nuts, explaining how they are grown, different ways to eat them, and how they keep you healthy"--Provided by publisher.
  ISBN 978-1-59920-336-2 (hardcover)
  1. Beans--Juvenile literature. 2. Cookery (Beans)--Juvenile literature. 3. Nuts--Juvenile literature.
  4. Cookery (Nuts)--Juvenile literature. I. Title.
  TX558.B4H43 2010
  641.6'565--dc22
                                            2008048172

WARNING: Some children may have an allergic reaction to nuts. Discuss this with children. Before eating or preparing any food, always check whether children have any food allergies, particularly to nuts.

9 8 7 6 5 4 3 2 1

Contents

What are Beans?

Beans are plant seeds that you can eat. They are sold fresh, canned, or dried.

fresh green beans

dried haricot beans

dried brown beans

lentils

Beans come in many different colors and sizes. Lentils are a very small type of bean.

These black-eyed beans have been added to a bowl of chili.

black-eyed bean

Beans can be used in lots of ways. They can be eaten hot or added to salads.

Canned Beans

Red kidney beans are sold canned or dried. They add color and flavor to a meal.

 Red kidney beans make soup more filling.

Garbanzo beans are small, round beans. They are often mashed to make a dip or cooked in a curry.

 Garbanzo beans cooked with red peppers make a delicious curry.

Green Beans

Green beans are the seed pods of a bean plant.

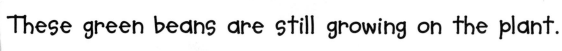 These green beans are still growing on the plant.

cooked green beans

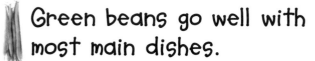 Green beans go well with most main dishes.

Fresh green beans are good for you. They can be boiled or steamed.

9

Bean Sprouts

Bean sprouts are the seedlings of plants. You can grow your own bean sprouts indoors.

A bean sprouting kit has a tray and seeds for you to grow at home.

Add crunchy bean sprouts to sandwiches or cook them in a delicious stir-fry.

Raw bean sprouts can be added to a salad.

Baked Beans

Baked beans are white beans cooked in a tasty tomato sauce.

Baked beans look like this before they are cooked and canned.

You usually buy baked beans in a can. They can be eaten as part of a main meal.

Try baked beans in a baked potato for a filling lunch or dinner.

What are Nuts?

Nuts are seeds covered with a hard shell. Most nuts grow on trees.

pecan nut

hazelnut

shell

walnut

almond

kernel

 You have to break the shell to eat the nut inside.

A handful of nuts and raisins is a healthy snack.

almond

raisin

walnut

hazelnut

brazil nut

cashew nut

 A packet of nuts and raisins is easy to put in your lunchbox.

Peanuts

Peanuts are sold in shells, without shells, salted, or dry-roasted.

dry-roasted peanuts

shell

peanut with skin on

peanut without skin

Inside the shell, peanuts are covered in a thin skin.

Crushed peanuts are mixed with oil and salt to make delicious peanut butter.

Try peanut butter on apple slices.

Cooking with Nuts

Nuts can be added to sauces, pasta, and stir-fries.

cashew nut

Cashew nuts make this stir-fry crunchy.

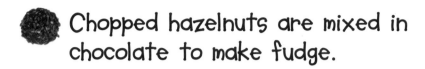 Chopped hazelnuts are mixed in chocolate to make fudge.

hazelnut

Nuts can also be used in cakes and desserts to add extra flavor.

Coconuts

Coconuts grow on palm trees. You can eat the white part inside the shell.

Shell

Meat

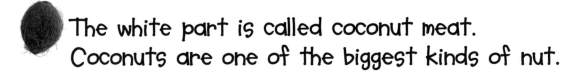
The white part is called coconut meat.
Coconuts are one of the biggest kinds of nut.

Coconut meat is crushed and made into coconut milk. This is used in cooking and drinks.

Coconut flakes are sometimes colored pink and used to decorate cakes.

Things to Do

Match the Food

Can you match the beans and nuts to the food made from them?

Pick a Nut!

Which of these foods are nuts? Can you remember what the nuts are called?

Sounds Tasty!

Match these foods to the descriptions below.

a) Crack open my shell and you'll find two smaller nuts.

b) Chopped and cooked, I go well with a main meal.

c) I can be colored pink and sprinkled on cake.

Glossary

curry A powder made from grinding spices that has a hot taste and is used to make meat and vegetable dishes.

seedling
A very young plant grown from a seed.

seed pod
The part of the plant where the beans or seeds are.

stir-fry
Chopped vegetables (or meat) fried quickly in a pan.

Index